Speed Reading

*Be More Productive, Remember More
and Improve Your Speed Reading With Exercises*

Victor Hawkins

Summary:

Introduction

Many people dread reading for any reason. They do not realize how beneficial it can be. Some people love reading for relaxation, but they hate reading for information. If you are one of these people, this is the book for you. It may seem a little redundant, a book on how to love reading again. However, this is the one you want to read. It will help you as you go on in life, whether you are in school, or you are an adult with a lot of reading to do for work. Read on to learn how speed reading can help you as you move through life.

What Is Speed Reading

Speed reading is a term that many people have heard before. However, not a lot of people are sure about what it means exactly. They think that it just means someone who reads really fast. They feel that speed reading is for people who are known to be "smart". This is not the case. We are going to dispel any rumors and myths there may be about speed reading in this chapter.

Myths

There are many different myths about speed reading. These myths can discourage several people from trying to use this valuable tool in their lives. Let us look at each one of those myths and work on reducing the stigma that surrounds speed reading.

Myth #1

"Speed reading is hard."

This could not be farther from the truth. Speed reading is a lot easier than most people realize, because you are only looking to read about specific information, rather than trying to remember every single bit of useless information you don't need. Speed reading makes it easier to retain information, and it takes a lot less time than reading a really large article.

Speed reading is really beneficial to those that have problems reading, and feel that reading is hard. There are ways that you can also enhance your speed reading abilities, and those will be gone over later on in this book.

Myth #2

"Speed reading is for smart people."

First, let's address the term "smart people". It is a common misconception that people who read well are smart, and people who do not are not as smart.

This is nowhere near being true. Reading and reading comprehension have nothing to do with being "smart". Modern society dictates that if you are not an extremely well-read person, you are not as intelligent as someone who is. However, they also put a huge strain on being mathematically inclined as well.

The truth is, generally people who are great at math may not be good at reading. The same in reverse. Not being great at reading does not mean that you are not smart, it simply means that you are not that great at reading. There is nothing wrong with that.

Speed reading is not for people who are extremely well-read, though they may use it to their advantage. Speed reading is actually designed for people who have trouble with literacy and being able to retain the information that they read. Speed reading was originally used by those who were slower at reading than their peers so they could keep up at the same pace knowledge wise.

Myth #3

"You have to be fast at reading."

This is not true at all. Even if you are a slow reader, you can still employ speed reading techniques. Speed reading has nothing to do with the pace you read at at all. The name may be a bit misleading, but the truth is, speed reading is used to help people who are slow readers get through the information at a higher pace without sacrificing information retention.

Speed has no bearing on being able to speed read. The term refers to how fast you are able to pull out the information due to not having to read every single bit of information that is on a given page.

Myth #4

"Reading every letter is important."

This is not true. Studies have shown that you do not have to read every letter to know what a word is. Your brain seeks out the first and last letter inherently and then fills in the rest. If you are trying to sound out every letter, that could be where your reading slows down.

Myth #5

"Slow reading makes for better comprehension."

A lot of people think that as you read, it helps to slow down to absorb the words into your memory. They feel that the slower they read, the better they will remember what they read. However, studies have shown that the opposite is known to happen.

Reading at a slow pace does not aid in comprehension at all. In fact, it hinders your comprehension, because you are too focused on each word to really put them together. Reading each word helps you understand each and every word that is on a page, however, you may have problems understanding what the text was truly about.

The reason for this is that you are going so slow, and by the time you get to the end of a paragraph, your brain completely forgets what the beginning of the paragraph was saying. If you find yourself having to re-read a paragraph over and over to understand everything, then you may be reading too slow. Later on in the book we will talk about how you can remedy the situation, and pick up the pace to aid in your information retention skills. There are many tips that will help you in this area though, so do not worry.

Myth #6

"Slow reading gives you more enjoyment."

This stems from the belief that slow and steady always wins the race. In reality, slow and steady just means you will finish with less exhaustion, however, you most likely will not come out on top. Especially when it comes to enjoying a book. When reading slow, as was discussed above, you are reading for comprehension of each word, rather than the piece as a whole. When you read a little faster, you will be able to make the words come to life.

Myth #7

"Speed reading is only for school aged children."

Most people associate speed reading with documents that are boring to read. This is not always the case. While it is more often used in this case, that is a specific type of speed reading. Regular speed reading is for everyone who reads anything. It helps you get through a book at a speed where you can truly enjoy reading, rather than finding it a chore. On the plus side, as an adult you can read a lot more of that novel, despite your busy schedule.

Types of Speed Reading

There are two major types of speed reading. Mostly in this book we are going to talk about the main one, which is just increasing your ability to read faster. However, there is a specialized form of speed reading that we will also touch on briefly for those who need tips on how to achieve the ability to take information out of a document without having to spend a lot of time reading.

Type #1

Basic speed reading

This is the type of speed reading where you read the entire document at a higher speed than you used to. It takes you to about 110-220 words read in a minute. This may seem like a lot, but considering the average person types around forty-five words a minute, and you can read twice as fast as you type, this is not extremely high. Some people can speed read at a pace of upwards of 350 words a minute. These are the speed reading pros who have been doing this most of their life.

Basic speed reading is the type of speed reading that people associate with those in higher literacy classes. In the high school years, it is the kid who could read four large novels a week on top of completing all of their homework. That is the basic speed reading, and while you may not be able to read that much due to time constraints as an adult, you too will be able to speed read with a little practice.

Type #2

Specialized speed reading

Thinking of speed reading, not a lot of people think about specialized speed reading, unless they think of school years. However, specialized speed reading can help you in adulthood as well. This is the type of speed reading that is used to retrieve information from a document without having to read the entire document from front to back. Reading this way requires the use of context clues, and intensified searching to help you find only what you need and ignore all of the rest of the information.

When To Use Speed Reading

There are several times when speed reading is helpful. You can use it pretty much any time you read once you get it down. There are some times when speed reading can be deemed more helpful than others, but that generally depends on the person. Here are a few ways that speed reading can be beneficial to you.

#1

Time constraints

You have a big project due for your company, and it involves a lot of reading, because you have to put a lot of research into this project. You want to impress your boss to try to get a promotion, so you decide to give it your all. The only problem is, the project construction will take about six days, and you only have seven in total. There is a lot of information to read, and you only have one day to read all of it on top of your other daily duties. You do not want to be up all night trying to squeeze the reading in, so you decide that you will try speed reading, which you haven't done in ages. You find that it works, and you manage to get the project done in a timely manner and impress your boss.

This is one scenario where you will find that speed reading is extremely beneficial, even if you use basic speed reading rather than specialized speed reading to finish the task. You have found that there is a lot of information that you were able to obtain in a timely manner. As an adult, it is hard to find a time where you can use speed reading. You feel that you do not really read enough to use it, however, any time you have to read anything is a chance to practice.

When you are in a pinch and have to read a lot in a short amount of time, speed reading can really be a beneficial tool for you to use. It will give you the boost you need to get the required reading done without infringing on your other daily duties. This will help you in the long run so that you do not feel like you are running out of daylight to do everything you need to do, and you will also not need to stay up later in the night to get everything done.

#2

Boring reading material

We all have those documents that we have to read for work or other important events in our life. These documents seem like they are not worth the time it takes to read them, but not reading them will cause you to miss out on the information you need. Whether it's for a business meeting, or a big event where you have to give a speech, or if you have to reply to an email on what you read. There are a lot of different times in adult life where you have to read something that you do not want to. The best way to do so is to read it as fast as you can so that you can get the information without having to waste a lot of time.

This is a good time for specialized speed reading if you know what information you are looking for. You can seek out that information and be done with the document in a few short minutes. However, if you do not know what information you are looking for, you may have a hard time with finding the right information. In this case, basic speed reading will be beneficial to you as you try to get through the uninteresting document.

#3

Novel reading

Picture this scenario. You have a novel that you absolutely love, but you don't have a lot of time to read. You find that by the time you pick up the book again, you have forgotten part of what you read because you are so busy. You never have time to read enough to really get into the plot line, so you just give up. Then a friend reminds you that sometimes the most enjoyable way to read is to speed read. You remember practicing speed reading a few years ago when you had a lot of reading to do in a short amount of time, so you decide to give it a go. Within a week you have finished the novel, and you remember the whole of the plot line.

Speed reading is not only for informational texts. It can be a useful tool when you are trying to read for pleasure as well, because you are not having to reread several sections just to move forward a little bit. You can get through more of the novel, and have more time to read because you can use any chunk of time to read, not just a day off, or a quiet evening at home. Your morning commute on the train becomes a viable fifteen minutes to get a chapter or two in.

When speed reading a novel, many people feel that it takes away from the enjoyment. This is not always the case. You can still let your mind get lost in the words, you just have to be more aware of your surroundings if you are not used to reading for short periods of time. Have a timer on your phone that will alert you to when it is time to find a stopping point in your book and focus on reality once more. You can enjoy a book no matter how long you spend reading it.

Even if it is only a few minutes at a time.

#4

Trouble concentrating for long periods of time

Over forty percent of the world's population suffer from an attention span disorder of some sort. These people have trouble focusing on one task for more than a few minutes at a time, and often find themselves having to reread a paragraph multiple times when they are reading. This is because their brain does not like to go slow and focus well.

You may be one of these people, and it may make you feel like you are not that good at reading, when in reality, you are just not very good at paying attention to things. Don't worry, speed reading can help with that, because instead of taking twenty minutes to read a body of text, you can get it done in five. Your brain will be happy that it does not have to focus for too long, and you will be glad that you are able to get some reading done so that you are not behind on work.

If you dread reading because you feel you are not good at it, that could be because you have trouble concentrating. You may shy away from speed reading due to this issue, but in reality, it should be the reason you run to it. You can help yourself by learning how to pull information from a text swiftly before your brain gets distracted by something else.

Speed reading is useful whether you are in school, or you are out in the work force. Any time you need or want to read something, you can use speed reading to get it done around your daily responsibilities. This makes it very flexible, and helps you so that you are not having to procrastinate because you dread the time it will take to read a certain body of text.

Basic Starter Tips

Speed reading is probably starting to sound interesting right about now. We have cleared up misconceptions, and talked about how it is relevant in life, even if you are an adult in the work force. Now that you know that it is possible to achieve, no matter your education level and where you are in life, you may be wondering how you can become a speed reader. You also may be wondering how you can get better at specialized speed reading for when you know the information you need and don't want to be walking around with useless information when you only need a certain amount. This chapter will get you started on how to speed read. Later on, we will talk about more in- depth tips on speed reading. We will also talk about how to retain the information that you have learned, and how to use time management along with speed reading to be more productive.

Let's start with the basics. When you are going

through this chapter, it is a good idea to have a body of text that you would like to read, so that you can practice as you learn. It could be a section of this book, or it could be something else entirely. Practice is important, because without it, knowledge is powerless.

Do not read each word separately

This can seem slightly confusing; however, the truth is it is fairly simple. All you have to do is read a group of words together. For example, if you see the words "she ate the apple" do not read it as "she" "ate" "the" "apple" with your finger following each word. Instead read the entire line like you would say it in a sentence. "she ate the apple". When you see simple words like the, and, a, etc. you want to make sure that you are not taking extra time to read them. They are just conjunctives and do not have any bearing really on your reading.

You can go from reading each word separately to reading blocks of words together by training your eyes to take in a line as a whole, rather than taking in each word separately. To do this, fixate your eyes on the line, rather than the beginning word. The brain is a wonderful thing, and you will soon learn that you can read the entire line without moving your eyes at all, and you can read it a lot faster, because your eyes are sending more information to your brain at once.

Here is a little piece of material for you to read. It is not anything that is very tough, just an excerpt so that you know how to practice for this tip. Start a timer before you start reading. When you finish the last line, stop the timer. It should not take you more than ten seconds to read this section of text.

The little boy was furious at his mother for not letting him sleep over at Joe's house. He wanted to scream, cry, and break things. However, he knew that was not the way to get her to change her mind. Instead he went to his room and began to straighten and tidy up. He took out the trash from his room, the bathroom, and the kitchen. He saw that there were dishes in the sink, and he washed them. He swept the floor and vacuumed the rug. When all that was done, he made sure that he had finished his homework, and that the dog was taken care of. By the time his mom came back downstairs from doing laundry, the house was tidy and neat. The little boy was on his feet in an instant, asking if his mom needed help with the laundry. "Nice try, but you are still not going tonight. It is family night."

This section of text is just a little over ten lines, and is full of fairly simple words so that you will not be tripped up by hard to pronounce words. It should only take ten seconds to read. If it takes longer than that, then you are not focusing on lines of words, rather single words or small blocks. Keep trying until you can read it all in under ten seconds.

When you are wanting to practice on your own, mark out ten lines of text in what you are wanting to read. Time yourself and try to beat ten seconds. The faster you can read ten lines, the better, because that equates to more time that you can do other things because you are not having to spend that time reading. When you do not have to spend too much time with what you are reading, you will find that it seems like less of a chore to do, and you will be more likely to want to get your reading out of the way so you can get on with other things during your day.

Blocking out your reading is one of the easiest ways to work on your reading speed, and it can even help with comprehension, because you are reading each line as a whole, rather than each word. This makes it easier to use context clues to figure out things that are confusing you, because you are reading the line all together. Unless you are trying to break down sentence structure, there is no need to read each word individually, because you are trying to gain comprehension of the text itself, not each word alone.

Do not focus on small words

Conjunctives and other small trivial words are not important. You are looking for three things in a sentence. Who, what, and why. Sometimes you need to know where as well, but that is rarely of importance. When you are reading for information, small words will just take up your time, and slow you down. For example, in the line "Sally ate an apple" you do not need the word an. You need the words Sally, ate, apple. That is it. The longer the sentence is, the better it will be for you to practice with, because there are more small words that can slow you down potentially.

Small words, and inconsequential details such as color, time, and distance are not necessary in most of your reading, unless you are reading for details. If you are just reading for general information, then you do not need to focus on the small words, and you can just go on to the big identifiers. This does not mean you do not read the small words, you just don't focus on them like you do with identifiers. In the English language, especially. it is tough to find out exactly what you need, but when you know, this tip comes in handy. Now let us move on to the exercise that will help you practice this tip.

In this next section of text, you need to be able to answer three things when finished. Who or what was the text talking about, what was going on in the text, and why it happened. You should be able to have that information in no more than five seconds. Set your timer, and begin.

The Twin Towers went down on September 11, 2001. This was a tragic day in history, because there were so many lives lost. The towers were struck down by enemy planes, and killed thousands of people, not only in the initial strike, but in the aftermath and rescue attempts as well. This lead to a devastation across America for weeks to come, and even sent the country into a war. The Towers were struck down by terrorists because the terrorists did not believe in the way Americans lived. They felt that freedom was a threat to them, because their people were getting ideas in their heads of freedom as well.

Okay. That is the text that we are working with. In five seconds you should have gotten this information. The Twin towers were destroyed by terrorists because the terrorists felt that the way Americans lived threatened them. That took nearly eight lines of text and shrunk it down into one single line. Notice that you did not need the date, or that thousands of people were killed. Those are outline details. Outline details are extra bits of information that can come in handy, but generally are not needed. Most of the time, you can just skim over those details, and temporarily store them while you focus on the plot line details. Plot line details are like the bread and butter of a story or text body. They contain the information that you need to know right then.

This is harder to practice on your own, so you may need a friend to help you. Have them read the text first and determine what information that you need to know, and then have them quiz you once you have finished reading. Try to get ten lines in five seconds. That is the main goal. Get the information you need in five seconds or less. Once you have mastered this, you will find that it is a lot easier to pull information out of a text body than you have ever experienced before.

Don't focus on one thing for too long

This seems like a given, but you would be surprised

how many people get hung up on unimportant things like pronunciation. The truth is, if it is a name or a place, you do not need to pronounce it right in the reading, because you can look it up later. You just have to know what is going on. Names and places do not really matter as long as you get the general idea.

For example, take the name Mrs. Gryzbowski. This is a very interesting last name, and seems like it would be hard to say. Rather than getting hung up on the name, you merely have to say in your head Mrs G. and move on. You do not have to pronounce the word in your head, you just have to know who you are referring too. Many people will stop with what they are reading to take the time to sound out the names rather than bookmarking that and moving on. The importance of moving on is to get your reading speed up. You may worry that not knowing the name will affect your comprehension, but it most definitely will not. You will have no implications on your comprehension whatsoever, because names have no bearing on the meaning of the text. Saying the full name or just Mrs. G, you still know that it is the same person, so there is no need to take the time to sound out the full name.

Here is a practice example, again you are going to do this like the first tip, and read ten lines in ten seconds. Here is the kicker, there are a few hard words in here that could cause you to stumble. If you can pronounce them, then that is great, if not, keep going, and when you are done reading, then you can get Google to pronounce the word to you for later reference. However, knowing the pronunciation doesn't matter unless you have to do a presentation on what you read.

So set your timer and get ready to begin.

Alyssius went on a tour of the National Kazakhstan museum. He found that it was very scintillating to learn more about the Khazakhstanian culture. He went with his class led by Mr. Kondratchyev. They toured the chapel area, and throughout all of the works of art that the museum held. The museum curator himself took them on the tour, and the entire class got to learn about every piece of Kazakhstan's history. It was wonderful for them to learn something so fascinating and so cultural, rather than learning about a culture they already knew pretty much everything about. The tour was a fun adventure for the class, and Alyssius was so glad he was able to go. He could not wait to get back to the museum at a later date to spend more time ogling the pieces of art and architecture.

This piece of text had a few harder words in it. You can always go back afterward to see how they are pronounced. However, they have no bearing on the comprehension of the piece. If you came across a word that did have a comprehension standpoint, you should be able to use context clues as you are reading to figure it out. You probably discerned that scintillating meant interesting if you did not already know that. However, most of the words in this piece were names of people or places.

If you did not read this in ten seconds or less, then you were allowing yourself to get hung up on the words themselves rather than just using an abbreviation and moving on with the text. You want to stop yourself from taking the time to focus on every single word, and that includes pronunciation. You should be reading in your head anyways, so if you mess up, no one will know. Comprehension, not pronunciation is what is important.

Those are some basic tips on how start speed reading. Remember to always practice what you are trying to learn.

How To Speed Read Like A Pro

Now that you have the basics down, there are some more advanced tips to help you raise the speed in which you read. These tips will take you from basic speed reader to pro level in no time at all. When you are reading, you may feel like your pace is fast enough, and if you are able to read the required material and still have plenty of time left over to get other things done on your to do list, then you may be at a pace that works for you. However, if you happen to get a heavier work load, it never hurts to be able to raise your speed just a little bit.

Complacency is a speed reader's worst enemy. Unlike with riding a bicycle, if you do not use speed reading, your reading speed decreases exponentially. You can raise it back up with a little bit of practice, but it is like losing a grade level in your education. Keep practicing even when you do not need it, and always work to improve your speed so that you have a reason to practice. The more reason you have to practice, the better you will be, and the faster you can read. You will find that reading becomes enjoyable, and you no longer dread reading for work. You look forward to learning new information, and being able to bring something to your business from what you learned. The faster you read, the more quality you will have when it comes to other aspects of your life such as time management, especially if you have to read regularly for your job.

Prioritize your reading

This may seem a little odd when it comes to speed reading, but it absolutely works. Not only for speed, but also for comprehension, because you know what is most important and what is least important. When you know those aspects, you know what you need to focus on so that you can comprehend the important parts of what you are reading. This works for when you are reading for work or even for leisure. Find what is most important to you and read it.

When you are prioritizing your reading, generally

leisure books are at the bottom. This is because they generally do not have useful information in them. However, sometimes you need a little time to relax rather than work all the time. You them will need to take some time and prioritize leisure reading. By doing this, you are also getting in practice for speed reading important documents as well. It may seem a bit odd to prioritize leisure reading, so make sure that you are not putting it above important documents for work, because it will be harder to focus on what you are currently reading if you are worried about something that is potentially more important.

This is another good reason to make certain things important in your reading list. That way, when you are reading something, you can focus on what you are reading, rather than worrying about if you are going to have the time to read something that could be more important than the text that you are currently reading. You want to be able to focus on what you are reading so that you do not have to keep rereading the same section over and over. You also want to be able to focus enough for adequate comprehension as well, because what is the point of reading something at a high speed if you do not understand what you are reading?

Read early in the day

This could possibly seem like an odd tip to use when you are trying to speed read. Who wants to do anything fast when they first wake up? It seems that no one could be of any use first thing in the morning. If this is what you are feeling, that is normal. However, it does not say, first thing in the morning, merely early in the day. You want to do your reading before you get into something else because you want to be able to focus on your reading. Also, without other problems that the day causes swirling in your head, it will be easier to concentrate on what you are reading, rather than worrying about the day's stresses like you would if you put the reading off till the end of the day.

When you wake up, eat breakfast, have your cup of coffee, or whatever your morning drink may be, and relax with your documents that you need to read. You will find that it is a lot easier to concentrate on what you are reading when you are relaxed, because your brain is not wanting to get distracted. This is also a good tip for those with attention deficiencies. You will find that early in the morning it is a lot easier to concentrate because your brain is still waking up, and is in a relaxed, almost sleepy state.

This makes this the optimal time to read those important texts and to start gaining comprehension on them. This also starts your day off well, because you are getting that out of the way before your day even starts, which leaves you with a full day to concentrate on other responsibilities. If you do not want to deal with worrying about your reading while working, this is a good tip.

So how does it help with speed? Simple, there are no distractions that will affect the speed of your reading in the morning, unless you have kids. If you have kids, it is best to wait till they are off to school first, or even take a "shower" to get the reading in. The tip has to do with allowing your brain to have a distraction free environment to thrive in.

Find the best environment

When reading for speed, you want to make sure that you are able to read as much as possible with as little strain as possible. This means strain on your eyes, brain, and body. If you are not in the right environment, you will find stressors will have an impact on your speed. You want to be in a comfortable area, but not too comfortable where you find yourself dozing off or daydreaming. A desk with a comfortable chair seems to be the best environment. You also do not want to have to lean over the text you are reading, because that can cause neck and eye strain. You want to have your text held at a forty-five-degree angle.

However, you do not want to have to hold the text if it is anything longer than a page to avoid strain on your wrist and forearms. A magazine or book stand will help prop the book up to help you avoid strain on your body.

How does this help speed? You will be able to focus solely on the text rather than how uncomfortable you are. This will help you to amp up your speed because you will be able to read the words and comprehend them without anything nagging in the back of your mind. You will not have to worry about discomfort or anything. It seems like a really weird tip, but it helps.

Take notes

Wait! How can you increase speed if you are stopping to take notes? It seems like it would be a little ironic when you want speed to stop and take time from the reading you are doing. The truth is, it is absolutely beneficial for people to take the time out to jot down a few brief notes. Especially if you are reading to answer questions later. Sometimes memory does not serve us well. In these cases, you want to make sure that you can jog your memory without having to reread the text over again. That is where notes come in handy. When reading, take a second after every section to take a few notes if there was something important on the page.

Your notes do not have to be extensive, they just have to be a basic synopsis of important facts. You can even jot down one liners to help jog your memory. You are not summarizing what you read, only making little place markers to help you remember when you need the information.

Taking the time to take notes prevents you from having to read the text once more, and saves you time in the end. Remember, no matter how fast you read, comprehension is what is most important.

Take a speed reading class

There are plenty of resources out there to help you get better at speed reading. There are classes online that you can attend for free, and websites to help you build your speed reading potential. You want to make sure that you are in some adequate online resources though, because some have tips that really are not beneficial.

A lot of speed reading online courses tell you to use a highlighter, when this is the opposite of helpful. It marks a place that you are too lazy to read so that you have to come back and read it later. Stay away from highlighters and write notes instead. If you have to highlight something, make sure that you read it well and put it in your notes so that you know why you highlighted it. The only time that you should have to highlight something is if you are saving it to reference it to someone else. Other than that, put the colorful see- through marker down.

Do not use a pointer

Many people will tell you that you should use a pointer when you are trying to speed read so you can keep your place easier. The truth is this will slow you down exponentially because it takes you back to having to focus on one word at a time. The goal is to not focus on one word at a time and focus on lines as a whole as was described in the basic tips chapter. You want to make sure that you can keep your place so just make sure that you are on the right line. A line marker may help in the beginning, because they are markers that just go down with each line you read rather than follow each word as you read it.

However you should be ditching the line marker as soon as possible, so that you can move through lines that much faster without having to pull the marker down. Once you start forgetting to pull it down and are still able to keep your place well, it is time for it to go. The reason for this is that you do not want anything slowing you down or distracting you when you are reading. Reading is a time to gain information, and anything that takes away from that should not be used when you are trying to read for speed.

When you are reading, make sure that you have all that you need for a comfortable experience. Some people have to be in a separate room so that they can concentrate with minimal distractions, some people like to have background noise. Neither one of those things are wrong, you just have to make sure that what you are trying to do is what really works for you. All that matters is you have a comfortable setting to read your documents and really get to understanding them in a timely manner.

Now that you have tips on how to become a great speed reader, you want to learn how you can retain more information and how you can help yourself comprehend more of what you are reading. The next chapter will go over these things to help you get even better at speed reading.

How To Retain Information

Speed reading is a useful tool when you use it right. However, if you cannot remember what you are reading, it does you no good at all. You have to be able to remember what you read when you are reading. This chapter is about how to retain information when you are reading so that you can adequately read at higher speeds.

When you are reading, you may find that remembering things that you are reading is difficult. That is because most of modern education teaches us to read for the moment, not for the long run, so remembering things is not as easy as you would think.

When you are reading, you want to be able to remember what you read. Earlier a tip was taking notes. This is a great tip, but there are more to help you out and they will also help you figure out what notes you should jot down as well.

Note taking is not the only tip that you can use to help you remember what you are reading. This chapter is filled with other equally important tips to help you adequately retain the important information that you need in order to be a successful speed reader.

Skim through the material

Take a moment to skim through what you are about to read. Look for important headings and subheadings. You do not want to read the actual text body yet, you are just looking for important things that you may need to remember. If there are any words that you need to know, make note of where they are in the text as well. You should not spend more than a minute skimming a ten-page text. You just want a base so that information will automatically stand out in your brain, and your brain will file that as important.

Skimming through the material is a great way to prepare your brain for reading as well. When your brain is ready, it is a lot easier for you to retain information that you are reading because the cortex of your mind is awake and active. You want to be alert when you are reading as well. It is best to skim the material first to tell your brain it is time to be awake and alert because it is time to learn.

Here is an example of skimming through some text. There is going to be a chunk of text offset by some headings and subheadings. There is also a bonus bolded word as well. Your goal is to make note of the heading, subheading, and bolded word in less than ten seconds.

Get your timer ready and begin.

> Cats are very interesting creatures. They can seem aloof, yet they also seem to need attention constantly. They are walking contradictions. You may find that cats are

hard to please, and demand food constantly. That is one of the many quirks a cat has. Here are some more of their quirks:

Territorial

Cats are very territorial, and they often have the need to mark their territory using their **pheromones**. Males do this by spraying a foul- smelling substance that resides in the glands around their anus, almost like a skunk. Females use the glands on their face and rub them where they have decided to mark their territory.

Marking Humans

You may notice that your cat loves to rub against your legs or your face. They do this because they are marking you as their territory. Both males and females mark humans this way. They also mark other cats as part of their group this way as well.

Above, you should have noted the heading "Territorial", the subheading "Marking Humans" and the important word "pheromones". Once you have this information, you will be able to find what information is important in these sections, because they will stick out at you. You can also look up the definition of the bolded word before you begin reading so you know the importance of it if you did not know it already.

Skimming through text will help you determine what information is important. It is especially helpful when you are only looking for certain information so you do not have to wade through pages of useless information to get to what you need to know. Such as the introduction in the text above. You could nearly skip over that completely and just go straight to the first heading.

Pose a question

This can be done while you are skimming the text to help you comprehend what you are reading. At the beginning, you pose a question that needs to be answered and you answer it by reading the text. This will help aid in retaining information because you are not only reading the text, you are putting it to use in real time. You are making your brain actively work with the information that you are feeding it, rather than the information just sitting dormant in your mind.

When you pose a question, make sure that it is one that actually needs answered. To do this, think of what you are needing to know from that body of text. How can you apply that information to what you are doing with the document you are needing to read, and pose the question from there. You do not want to answer a question on useless information, you want actual knowledgeable information to stick with you. You do this by making sure that you are asking the right questions and getting the right answers.

In this example, you are going to pose a question at the beginning, and then read through the text to answer the question. It should only take you ten seconds to pose the question, and twenty seconds to read through the text and answer it. Get your timer ready, and begin.

Dogs are seen as a man's best friend, but are they really? Dogs are known to be vicious at times as well. Dogs are seen as less complicated than cats, but they come with their own set of complications.

Eagerness to Please

Dogs were domesticated to be working animals. They were not originally pets. This causes them to want to please their masters, because it is how their brains were trained. When a dog sees its

master, the dog immediately wants to make the master happy to avoid punishment, and possibly get a reward. Over time, dogs have developed to seeing the world of humans as their masters and began to develop a bond with them. This makes them even more eager to please, because to them we are the pack leader and their master.

Aggressiveness

Dogs can be aggressive if they were raised by a cruel owner. They, like humans, respond to trauma in many different ways. They remember when they are beaten and associate it with doing something wrong. Many dog fighting dogs do not want to be aggressive, it is just what pleases their owner, and eventually it is all they know.

Okay. From this text you should have formed the question somewhere along the lines of "how can an eagerness to please correlate with aggressiveness in dogs?" You get that information from the heading and the subheading, creating enough of a contrast to pose a very important question. After reading, you should have gained an answer along the lines of "dogs wish to please their masters so when in the wrong hands, they can be trained to be aggressive."

You can use this tip to also help you if you are writing notes as you go along. Do not write the question, merely write down the answer so that it will jog your memory on what you read about dogs. When writing notes, you want to keep them short. Using the question and answer method when it comes to note taking will make it a breeze. It will also keep note taking from eating into your time when you are speed reading.

Stay away from highlighters

We touched briefly on the problem with highlighters earlier in the book. However, that was on how it relates to the speed issue. Highlighters will cut down your speed because you have to go and read the topic over again rather than reading it once and moving on.

Highlighters also cause you to forget more than they help you remember.

That is because they mark your place so you can always find it, and your brain correlates that with not needing to remember it. You want to make sure that you are forcing your brain to remember what you are reading so highlighters are a bad idea all around.

Share the information

When you read something, your brain categorizes it. If you are not going to use it immediately, then your brain views the information as not important, so you do not remember things as easily. Find someone that you can share the information you just learned with so that your brain has something to do with the information. You also will hear yourself go over what you just learned driving the information that much further into your head. You can do this with regular reading or speed reading.

With speed reading, it is definitely important to do something with that information that you just received immediately because it is in your brain for less time than it would be if you were reading at a slightly slower pace. You want to use the information wisely, so make sure that you can share it with someone, or even just make a note to yourself.

Voice recording

When you are reading, instead of taking physical

notes, take audio notes. This way you are not only getting the information via your eyes, you are receiving it through an auditory fashion as well. Voice recording will help your mind really hold onto what you learned.

In the same way that sharing information helps you retain what you learned, voice recording does the same, and is really handy if you do not have someone to share it with. You can then play the notes back so that you can hear the information you have received.

Here is a section of text for you to practice all of these tips on. Skim the text, pose questions, answer the questions, do not highlight, and make notes. You do not need to time yourself, however if you wish to, the entire process should take no more than three minutes' tops. This includes making notes with whatever process you choose to do so with. When you are ready, begin.

Cell phone usage has risen exponentially in the last ten years. This could be due to the increase in technology along with the decrease in the cost of service. Whatever the reason, cell phones have become a staple in every household, and they are slowly becoming more and more powerful.

Increasing Cell Phone Usage

In the beginning, only wealthy families had a cell phone, and even then, it was only for emergencies. As a few years went by, cell phones became more commercially available to middle class families. The use of cell phones started to increase slightly, but they were still not used for much more than emergency. Most middle- class families only had one cell phone for the entire household.

However, as time wore on, more and more families started using cell phones, and the age of technology was born. Prices went down as technological advances increased.

Smartphones

Smartphones eventually came on the market around 2007. At first, they were extremely expensive, and did not have a lot of options other than a basic web browser and a touchscreen, however, as scientists found ways to improve on the functions of the phones, they also found ways to make them cheaper, and even made using the plans cost less. Now it seems like every family in the world has a smartphone, even lower class families tend to have at least one smart phone per household.

You can decide for yourself what are important questions in this text. This is just a practice to get you started moving along.

Time Management

Speed reading is great for helping you manage your time and being more productive if you use it correctly. You want to make sure that you are properly scheduling each day around what you have to read so that you have the proper amount of time to do everything.

You may be wondering why managing your time has anything to do with speed reading at all, but the truth is it has a lot to do with your ability to read pretty well. The reason speed reading is important is it helps you get on with your day without having to take a huge chunk of time to read some things for work or whatever else you have to read for. If you do not manage your time wisely, you will have no time to read, so even speed reading is not helpful in that case.

Before we go into tips on how to manage your time for adequate productivity levels, let's discuss why time management is important at all. Knowing why time management is important will make it a lot easier to understand why it is that you need to manage your time when it comes to speed reading.

#1

The number one reason that time management is important is stress relief. Have you ever had a day where it seems that there are not enough hours in the day to get done what you need to get done? It can cause a lot of stress. These are the times where time management are the most important. If you are not able to manage your time wisely, then you cannot adequately get things done in a timely manner. This leads to a lot of unnecessary stress on your day. It can also cause you to procrastinate even more, because your brain just does not want to deal with the stress.

When you manage your time wisely, then you will have time to breathe even on your busiest days. This will allow you to relax a little, and make sure that you are not having any issues with getting things done. The more relaxed you are, the easier it is to tackle things that are important, because your brain is prepared for what is coming your way. You will not go into panic mode which can send you into fight or flight mode.

#2

Managing your time allows you to have more time to yourself. This is important for your mental health. If you spend all of your time working, and never get to have any time to relax, then your body begins to wear out, and your mind will break down. This can lead to you getting physically sick, or can even cause a mental breakdown. When the body is under stress constantly, it can cause some serious problems. You also may have more trouble sleeping if your day seems really unorganized and busy. This is because it takes the body longer to fall asleep after a really busy and stressful day.

When your body is constantly going, it will not be ready to rest. You want to make sure that you have a to do list so you know exactly what needs to be done each day, so that you can manage your time accordingly.

#3

You can get more things done. This is one of the perks that not a lot of people realize. When you approach your day in an organized manner, you will find that you may have more time in the day than you realized. You can use that time to be more productive, and get a few more things done so that your next day is less stressful. Forget the phrase "why do today what you can put off till tomorrow" and just get it done. When you have the time, do it. This will make it easier to get in a routine and make you more likely to stay with planning your day successfully.

#4

You become less likely to forget things. When your day is organized, you will find that it is a lot easier to remember things. The reason this happens is that your brain is not so busy trying to figure out what all needs done that it forgets things that may seem not as important. You want to be able to remember all of the things that you learned that day, so being organized is of utmost importance. You also will be more likely to get everything done that you need to that day, because you will be less likely to forget tasks that seem menial compared to what other tasks you may have gotten done that day.

When you are organized, your memory increases tenfold, because your brain can focus on what needs to be memorized, rather than everything else going on. It is nice to have a clear head when you are reading, so you should be sure to manage your time wisely. When you are organized, you will find that you don't forget where you put your car keys or your wallet. You will find that remembering what you were going to need from the store is easier as well. Your minor memories will be easier to obtain just from a simple thing like planning your day well.

#5

You will find that your quality of life improves. Everyone wants to have a happy and care free life, however, if you are unorganized, you will have an issue with being able to have a care free attitude. It will feel like you are uptight all of the time. None of this is conducive to a good reading environment, let alone a good life environment. You want to have a calm atmosphere around you. Not only when reading, but when doing daily tasks as well. You will find that you feel better and you are able to do more things, and have more energy if you are not dreading each day.

Tips for managing your time

Now that you understand why it is important for you to manage your time wisely, here are some tips for you to use when you start managing your day. You want to do this as much as possible, not only when you have reading to get done, because you want to be able to work your day around any reading that needs done, and if you are unorganized, that gets harder to do. You want to go through life with the right tools to get things done, so you should make sure that you are organized each and every day. You want to be more productive as well, and this will help with that.

Get a daily planner

This may seem a little juvenile to you, but a lot of professionals use them as well. Now people have apps on their phones to help them organize each day, and most calendar apps can do that. There are also to do lists that you can add alarms to so that you know when things should get done. Even a paper planner is better than nothing. The reason a planner is a good idea is because you can see what needs to be done, and you can allot time slots for what needs to be done, not just write a to do list and not have a schedule to go with it.

You want to make sure that you are using the planner daily, so that you can get used to scheduling each day out. You will find that it makes life easier to see exactly what needs to be done, and when you will do it. You may feel like you are becoming a robot controlled by time, but it makes life a lot easier to handle. The ease of using a planner makes it worth the purchase, as a paper one is generally only a dollar.

Apps you can get for free, however, if they crash, you may not know what to do.

Know your time

One of the hardest things about being organized is that you can know what you need to do, but getting it done in a timely manner is a whole different ball game. A lot of times, if you do not have specific time constraints, procrastination kicks in, and makes you slack off, causing you not to get everything done that you wanted to. You need to make sure that when you are making a to do list, you have times for each project that you need to do. Make sure that you work diligently to ensure that you get everything done on time. If you go over, make sure that you work harder on the next task so the domino effect does not kick in.

The domino effect is when you run over your time limit with one project, and it makes you run behind on everything else if you do not pick up the pace with the next project. You want to prevent this from happening, because a few minutes adds up fast. You want to be sure that you are getting everything done on time so that you do not have to cut into your breaks to get everything done.

Knowing how much time to allot yourself for each project is important so you do not try to overbook yourself. It is better to give yourself a few extra minutes than to give yourself too little time to get everything done with quality. This can cause a lot of issues and makes scheduling your day seem like a waste of time, because you are still stressed. The point of scheduling your day is to remove stress.

Allow for breaks

Most people feel that they will do better if they work straight through and do not have a break. They feel it will give them more time to get projects done. However, your body and mind needs to be able to have some time to recoup from strenuous work. Allowing yourself even a few five-minute breaks is better than working straight through all day. You will actually be more productive if you take breaks often. However, if you do not allow yourself to take a break, you will begin to slow down significantly.

Breaks are not a sign of weakness, it is you taking care of your body. Go to the restroom, drink some water, eat a snack, and just rejuvenate your mind and body in general. Also, do not skip breakfast or lunch just to get more work done. You need food to refuel your body so that your mind can function properly. Without the proper fuel, you will begin to feel tired, and like you can't keep going. This is because you are running out of energy. The truth is, your body needs food. Even if it is just a quick snack, or healthy protein shake, you need to give your body the nutrients it needs to help you be successful. Not doing this does not aid your success at all. In fact, it is counterproductive. You are trying to save time, but in the long run you will take more time to get things done.

So how does all of this apply to reading? Remember when we talked about how if you do not have to stress about your day, you can focus on reading? This is how you avoid stressing about your day. It also aids in memory retention, and comprehension, because your brain can be more focused. If you are focused, and in the zone, then you will find that you can read a lot faster, and gain more information than you ever thought possible. Productivity is important when you are wanting to be a speed reader. When you prioritize your day, you will find that your day gets easier, and your mind is sharper.

Subvocalization is quite common among all readers. It is all about saying words in the mind as you read, and also it is one of the main reasons why most people have slow reading speed. It also makes it difficult to improve one's reading speed. There are plenty of speed-reading programs that tend to exaggerate and falsely claim that the primary key to increasing your reading speed is to discard subvocalization. But it has been found from various studies that elimination of such a habit completely is impossible. We will discuss the way in which readers can reduce subvocalization in this section. As you minimize your subvocalization tendencies, you can easily boost up your speed of reading. In fact, it can help in enhancing your comprehension.

Do You Hear Voices in Your Mind While Reading?

When we were taught to read during our childhood days, we were told to read everything aloud. As you got fluent enough, your teacher might have told you to say the words that you read in your mind. It is the way in which the overall habit of subvocalization tends to originate in general. The majority of people keep reading in this way for their whole lives. However, if you are willing to increase your reading speed, you will have to reduce such a habit. There is no need to say every word that you read in your mind to understand the meaning. When you were young, it was important to repeat every single word in your head. However, with growing age, you can now determine the meaning of the words simply by looking at them. You are no longer required to pronounce the words aloud in your mind in order to get the same kind of understanding.

But there might be situations when you tend to read without saying the words in your mind. For instance, think of the times when you drive. As you see a red signal, do you tend to subvocalize the word "stop" in your mind? You must have done so in the moment ass you read the word in the sentence; however, as you come across a stop sign at the time of driving, your chances of saying the word are nil. You have a glance at the sign and recognize it automatically that it is a sign to stop. In case you are like the majority of readers, you might subvocalize most or all of the words in the mind. However, you might not subvocalize all the time everything that you read.

Let us have a look at one more example.

Suppose you are reading something and come across the yea "1987," you would not say in your mind "Nineteen Eighty-Seven." You are most likely to understand the year simply by having a glance at the number. Or, in case you come across the number "3, 546, 789," you would not subvocalize the same into words. For such a number, you have a look at it, and you can understand that it is a big one. Such an understanding comes quite quickly. There is no need to subvocalize the number. But if you do, you will be staring at the number for quite some time without making any kind of progress in the sentence.

It Is All About Ideas

Reading has nothing to do with words. However, it is all about the extraction of ideas, getting details, and absorbing necessary information. Words themselves might not mean anything unless they come surrounded by some other words. As you read "New York City," do you think of it as three separate words? The majority of us would just equate the words to a city. In fact, NYC would indicate the same thing. Right? We see several words that are only used for grammar, such as a, an, the. They would not provide you with the same kind of meaning as the word "college." You need to reduce subvocalization to boost up your reading speed. But what is the reason behind this? It is because subvocalization can easily limit how fast someone can read.

You can think of it in this way – if you say every word in your mind, does not that indicate that you can only read at the speed at which you can talk? In case you tend to say every word in your mind, your limit will be the speed at which you talk.

Reading Speed Is Equals to Talking Speed

The average speed of reading for most of us is about 160 – 250 words every minute. The average speed of talking is more or less the same. As most people say words in their minds as they read, they tend to read at a similar rate in which they talk. It is possible to test it out on our own. Try to read normally for one minute, and then try to read out loud for a minute. In case you are like most people, your talking speed and reading speed will be the same. If the speed at which you read exceeds the speed of talking, that is a great thing. No one wants to get limited to his/her talking speed. What is the reason behind most people reading around 150 – 250 words per minute and not anything above 300? It is because it is tough to speak that fast.

Unless you are habituated to disclaimers that can be found at the end of commercials, it is not at all easy to speak more than 300 words every minute. So, you need to minimize subvocalization to avoid getting stuck with reading as fast as you speak. In fact, you have got the power to read as fast as you think. Altering the habit of subvocalization is much easier said than being done. You cannot turn down the voice in your mind. In place of trying to eliminate the habit, you can desire to reduce the same.

How Can Subvocalization Be Useful at Times?

Repeating and saying words in your mind can be useful at times. For instance, as you read some material that involves technical vocabulary or terminology that you are not used to. In such situations, as you repeat words in your mind or even say them aloud, it can be a great way to enhance and expand your vocabulary. There is another way in which subvocalization can be useful. In case you need to memorize something word by word, trying to subvocalize the related words or saying the words aloud can help. How do you think that the actors remember the long dialogues? It is all done with the help of subvocalization. Reading out loud can help in memorizing something word by word.

However, when you read normally, you will rarely need to know something by every word. The majority of the time, you read is to extract ideas, information, and necessary details. In order to boost up your speed of reading, you will have to reduce subvocalization by trying to say only some words in every line. In case you try to say every word, you will get limited to the talking speed. But how will you know that the habit is changing? If you start with reading 3oo words every minute, you can be clear that you are saying every word in your mind, and that is why the word count is low. However, if the count goes up to 400 words per minute, you can regard it as definite progress.

Ways of Minimizing Subvocalization

Here are certain tips that you can follow.

Using your hand to guide the eyes at the time of reading

You must have heard experts stressing to use your hand so that you can guide your eyes. Well, it can be regarded as a primary principle of all kinds of speed-reading techniques and is very effective that can help reduce subvocalization. As you use your hand to guide your vision, it can help in grabbing a number of words at the time of reading, whereas helping you to deal with another habit of reading – fixation.

Distracting yourself

In order to minimize subvocalization, you can try to distract yourself from saying all the words in your mind. But how can someone distract themself? There are certain ways of doing this. One of the best ways is to have chewing gum as you read. It will prevent you from repeating words in your head. Also, subvocalization is not only about the inner voice. Your tongue, ears, larynx, and lips all play some role in the overall process. But if you can distract all such organs, you will be able to reduce subvocalization. You can distract your ears while reading with light music. Stay away from loud music. You can keep your larynx occupied by soft humming with the music.

Scanning before reading

To reduce subvocalization, it might be useful to master complex words or unfamiliar terminologies. The main idea is to scan the available text quickly before you decide to get into detail. One of the ways of doing this is to perform a super quick scan using your fingers and draw an "S" shape across and down the whole page. You will have to force the eyes to track the tip of your finger. The main aim of such a scan is not to gain insight; however, to pick up all kinds of unfamiliar terms and words. As you come across one, subvocalize it deliberately. As you start reading, your chances of subvocalization will be less.

Occupying the inner voice with some other thing

As it is not possible to eliminate subvocalization completely, the best thing that can be done on your part is to keep your inner voice busy with other tasks. One of the simplest ways of doing so is to count in your mind as you start reading. As you keep counting 1, 2, 3… in your mind while reading, your inner voice will not get enough time to pay attention to the text that you are trying to process. It might seem a bit tough in the starting; however, after some time, you will realize that you can read faster without even finding the repetitive list distracting.

The Technique of Reduced Margin

The majority of printed material that we come across has margins – the space that lies between the actual text on the page and the edge of the page. When online articles first came into being, the programmers of the websites underestimated the necessity of margins on the part of readers. They ended up populating the website with pages that included no margins at all. After a few years, it was clear that margins can very well impact the readability of any form of digital text. Margins were then added to all kinds of websites and templates. Indeed, margin-less pages on the internet can still be found, but it is clear today that including wide white space around any kind of text is necessary for readability.

Reduced Margin

As we already said that margins are necessary, then why is it needed to reduce the same? Although having margins is necessary for easy reading, you need to realize that they do not have any text and so there is no need for sharp foveal vision. Peripheral vision can do all the tasks as all that you need from margins is to determine where lines start and end. In order to take complete advantage of your peripheral vision on text margins, you can start to move in or indent the initial and final fixations on every line. You need to do this intentionally. For making it look easier, try to think of two vertical lines that run down the page right over the text, half an inch from the outward area.

Here is the way in which the eye movement of a reader alters as they use the technique of reduced margin. Below are two lines with and without the technique of reduced margin. If each of the highlighted areas denotes a fixation, is it possible for you to guess which one is which?

The weather improved after the drought, and the weather was looking promising for the crops.

The weather improved after the drought, and the weather was looking promising for the crops.

Try to note that the first example has only four fixations, whereas the second one has six. Naturally, you can read the first sentence faster. With this, you can realize that the first example used the technique of reduced margin and the second example did not.

The Parafovea

The technique of reduced margin needs the activation of a new eye area, the parafovea. It is like a thin belt that can be found around the fovea, the retina part that is generally used for reading. Well, it is not that sensitive to details like the fovea. Also, it cannot distinguish words. But the parafovea comes with the capability to detect shapes and is superior to the other eye parts. The retina consists of another external belt known as the perifovea. It also plays the part of peripheral vision. Parafoveal vision is a peripheral vision that utilizes the area of parafovea area – found between the fovea and perifovea. It is involved in the function of determining fixations.

As it comes with the ability to detect shapes, the parafovea can very easily read the word shapes and clusters. It makes predictions regarding a better landing for the upcoming eye fixation. As you optimize your fixations, you will be able to reduce the number of stops on every line. Thus, you can also maximize your comprehension. Keep in mind that the development of parafoveal vision requires time along with lots of training. It is similar to any new habit. So, you can practice using your material for a couple of months so that you can achieve noticeable improvement. As you start, you can draw vertical lines using a pencil so that you can remind your brain to reduce the margins.

Advanced Parafoveal Reading

You can utilize the retinal periphery area not only to reduce the number of fixations on every line; however, also to preview the available material ahead. As you read some text, your eyes view the spaces and words that are present on the current line. The brain and retina capture two or three lines that are outside the area of foveal vision. You can effectively tap into this info so that you provide yourself with the needed help to preview the text lying ahead. You can also plan the fixation stops. As already said earlier, perifoveal and parafoveal vision are not that sharp like the foveal. However, they can still register the boundaries and shapes of the words quite well. Certain words, such as "occasionally" and "knowledge," come with a particular shape along with length. Prepositions, such as "at," "in," and "of," are short in size that is surrounded by white spaces. They can also signify the starting of a cluster. With continuous practice, the brain can be made better to register them with the help of peripheral vision and also adjust the movements of the eyes accordingly.

The Technique of Word Clustering

It has been found that readers who read fast tend to cluster words. It is also assumed that if slow readers can learn the ways in which they can fixate on two or three words at one time, they can also read and understand any kind of text much faster. But it does not function that way. Lesser frequent stops every line is not the primary reason behind the faster speed of reading. Speed readers possess some excellent skills for processing language. So, mastering the technique of word clustering need to start with improving your skills of visual language processing.

To start with, let us learn some simple word clusters or sets of words that can develop some meaning as a group. Such a technique is universal and can help you to enhance your skills regardless of your present reading speed. Some simple examples of word clusters can include phrases, such as "in the night," "of the test scores," and "at the center."

All the phrases in the example start with a preposition and end with a noun. In English grammar, all such word clusters have a name that can speak for itself – prepositional phrases. You can also call them prepositional clusters.

Quick Exercise

You will have to identify six clusters in the following paragraph. You need to find them out by drawing brackets around the clusters in your mind. It is important that you not only spot the prepositions but also outline the boundaries of the cluster. Keep in mind that they will always start with a preposition and will end in a noun.

At a beach, individuals relax with several activities – jumping over the ocean waves, lying in the sun, and enjoying with friends.

Answer: (At a beach), individuals relax (with several activities) – jumping (over the ocean waves), lying (in the sun), and enjoying with (their friends).

If you create larger clusters, such as (lying in the sun) or (jumping over the ocean waves), that is a great thing as it indicates that you can see large word sets that can create some meaning together. Here is another practice piece where there are about seven prepositional clusters.

In this harmonica class, you will learn from one of the experienced teachers at this music school. She started her training at the age of six when she insisted on taking lessons in harmonica with her elder brother. Now, she boasts about 20 years of experience in teaching harmonica.

Answer: (In this harmonica class), you will learn (from one of the experienced teachers) (at this music school). She started her training (at the age of six) when she insisted on taking lessons in harmonica (with her elder brother). Now, she boasts about 20 years (of experience in teaching harmonica).

Prepositional clusters are quite simple to spot and can also provide you a better sense of what is more important in a sentence. You will be able to find out the secondary portions of a sentence. For instance, the main "action" and "actor" of the sentence, the verb and the subject, can never be seen in a prepositional cluster. All those words that tend to carry some essential meaning will be positioned outside the cluster.

Advanced Technique of Word Clustering

Let us take your knowledge of meaning and words to an

advanced level. One of the most frequently used words that can be found in the English language is the article "the." It is a word that opens most of the written sentences. Well, the reason for this is quite obvious – the majority of sentences start with the subject, which is typically a noun that requires an article. So, if you find out an article with a capital "T," you can be certain that the main actor or subject of the sentence will follow. Such kind of recognition of this sign can provide you all the help to cluster words in an intelligent way in place of doing the same accidentally.

Try to cluster some of the words in the following paragraph.

The path became narrower. Because of the flowers, both of us started to sneeze, and we went in the opposite direction of the Columbus Circle. The allergies made us get back to the hotel room. The trip to the nearest medical shop helped; however, we did not feel like getting back to the blooming park for the next two days.

Answer: (The path became narrower). (Because of the flowers), both of us started (to sneeze), and we went (in the opposite direction) of the Columbus Circle. (The allergies) made us get back (to the hotel room). (The trip to the nearest medical shop) helped; however, we did not feel like getting back (to the blooming park) (for the next two days).

Try to notice that when any sentence does not start with an article, it usually starts with an opening cluster, such as "Because of the flowers." Such a phrase will be offset by a comma and will get followed by the subject of the sentence. Such a trick can be used to deal with comprehension and also for locating the primary actor of a sentence if it is not present at the starting.

Conceptualization and Visualization

Visualization is the necessary power to develop mental imagery and to improve your performance along with learning. Visual imagery is common for memory, imagination, and daydreaming. However, there are people who find it tough to take up such visual images. Due to this, they tend to face difficulties in performing or learning any kind of activity. Not being able to draw up mental images is termed "congenital aphantasia." Keep in mind that mental imagery plays an essential role in getting to know new meanings and for reading comprehension. Mental imagery can provide you with all the help to take in concepts of all kinds of abstract things. With the usage of mind maps, you can keep and recall necessary info.

How to Opt for Effective Visualization?

Visualization helps in enhancing the skills of reading comprehension so that you can acquire more info through text understanding. We can visualize text automatically as we keep practicing using such a skill. As you visualize while reading, you will get the chance to acquire a good reading experience and keep in mind everything you read. When an individual hears or reads some sort of text by visualization, they can link themselves to the actual text. For instance, all those who read storybooks can get engaged with the characters of the story as they can truly think about the characters. Such a thing can help them to get the experience of proper reading besides getting all the encouragement to continue reading the book. It is quite easy to get started with practicing visualization. All you need to do is to choose a text that consists of descriptive languages and strong verbs.

You can start from a portion that will provide you all help to conjure detailed images. Well, there is no requirement to get involved in a complete book at the starting. You have got the choice to opt for some properly structured sentenced or any paragraph so that you can start with the lesson of visualization. There are certain strategies that can be followed.

Reading

You can enhance your skill of visualization with independent reading, listening to any text, or by being a part of reading activities in any small group. Also, you can turn off the lights and close your eyes to listen. It will help you in visualizing even more. It is possible to opt for frequent pauses so that you can share mental images as you read within any group. The textbook also holds some important functions in enhancing the ability to develop visual images. It is always advisable to opt for a book that has zero or fewer pictures. A professional writer will use descriptive language, which can provide the readers all the help to develop mental images of their own.

Exposure

Our minds can develop visual images involving all those things which are already stored there. In case you want to opt for effective visualization, it is necessary to expose yourself to experience variable things. You will need to read books, watch videos, and opt for various kinds of activities. Doing so will help the mind to establish realistic and detailed visual images.

How to Make Visualization Simple?

Visualization is not that tough. Any individual can fulfill their dreams when they try to determine a feasible path. You have got the power to feel and see all those things that you create in your mind with the help of visualization. As you hear, read, or feel anything, it can provide you the necessary help to develop mental images by following the process of visualization.

Regular practice of visualization

Repetition is one of the best ways in which you can acquire the power for visualization. It is necessary to visualize on a daily basis. Also, keep in mind the schedule that you need to follow. You can opt for any time of the day to practice daily visualization. However, the time after and before sleep is regarded as the perfect time. You will have to maintain some sort of consistency to build mental images. All of this will help you to visualize in a detailed and better way.

Deciding on visualization practice

It does not even matter where you are. It is possible to start with the practice of visualization any time and anywhere. However, it is necessary to experience some feeling of relaxation as you practice visualization. As you choose the desired goal, you will be able to develop a natural image that too within a constricted area. After that, you will have to try to expand all your thoughts by feeling the atmosphere around you. Such a technique can also help in the reduction of anticipatory anxiety.

Imagining yourself in a targeted area

Anyone can practice visualization simply by thinking about their existence within a specific region. It is a useful technique that can help to deal with fear and anxiety, which you might feel about a certain matter. You will have to try to walk yourself into an embarrassing step slowly. For instance, you might feel nervous about giving a speech in front of others. If you can get started by visualizing yourself giving your speech in front of others, it can easily develop a comfortable feeling. You will feel easier to speak in front of other people.

Practicing reading with images in mind

Visualization can help in enhancing the skills of comprehension and memory. Making a picture story depending on the subject you have read can help.

Visualization for Comprehension

As you start to read as a beginner, or you feel it is tough to read, you will need to learn visualization techniques so that you can master the skills of reading comprehension. With the application of visualization, people can develop story images that they read. As a reader, you input all forms of senses, like sound, smell, taste, touch, and sight, as you read any comprehension and use skills of visualization for the formation of mental images. You can concentrate on any kind of text as you form mental images. Visualization permits readers to retain the text info within the memory. You can apply various visualization methods for the creation of mental images of comprehension that you read.

Listening and then reading

It is considered a superb strategy to listen to a text when someone else is reading that aloud. After that, you need to try to develop some images regarding what you hear. Then, you can highlight or mark the text portions, which helped you to develop the mental images. Listening carefully is an important aspect as it can assist in learning various things, like languages, integration of previous stories, and many others. Reading and listening are connected strongly. As you improve your listening skills, you will be able to enhance your skills of comprehension, which will provide you with better reading skills. Keep in mind that there are two factors that can influence a person's level of reading. They are background knowledge and vocabulary knowledge. When you have a wide collection of vocabulary, it can provide you with all the help to read and comprehend the text's meaning.

Opting for some auditory piece

You might face trouble hearing or recognizing some words as you read any text. So, it is necessary to select an auditory piece, which can be a nursery rhyme, poem, any popular song, or a paragraph. It can provide you with a lot of details that you need for the skill of visualization.

Selecting some element for concentration

You can opt for some particular text or story with strong descriptive characters and settings. It can help you to focus and also apply your power of visualization to get to know the meaning of the text or story.

Visualization Exercises

There are some easy visualization exercises that will let you enhance your capability of imagination besides improving your creativity.

Object exercise: You will need to observe some objects properly. It will help in thinking about that object with your eyes closed. After that, you will need to visualize considering various angles by rotating the object using your mind. You will also have to pay attention to the object's surroundings.

Picture exercise: In this, you will need to examine one picture properly and then develop some image in mind after closing your eyes. You will need to try and recall the colors, background, surroundings, and everything possible about the picture. After that, you will need to look at the picture once again so that you can compare it with the visualization.

Place exercise: In this exercise, you will have to think about the environment where you currently exist. After that, you will have to pay attention to the selected environment. If you are willing to make the visualization seem more original, you will need to involve your senses so that you can focus on observing the object.

In fact, you can also include the sounds and smells in relation to the picture.

Person exercise: You will need to select an individual who is well-known to you. After that, you will have to draw one picture of the person within the eyes of your mind, taking into consideration various locations and situations. You can include facial expressions of the related person within your picture. You can repeat all these to exercise various individuals.

Controlling Eye Movements

In general, parents and doctors call it ADHD/ADD when someone feels it is tough to pay attention or cannot learn anything. It might be the result of improper eye movements. Due to this, an individual might face difficulties in various areas, like writing, reading, sports, etc., when your eyes cannot move precisely, efficiently, and accurately. When someone suffers from a poor form of eye movement, that person will find it really tough as they try to visualize something. There are two types of eye movements that are associated with visualization.

Saccades: We have already discussed these in the previous chapters. These are jerk-like movements of the eye that helps in altering visual focus as you see various things. It can explain your visual skills.

Pursuits: As you track something, you will need to pursue the object's movement by using all your skills of visualization.

For resolving issues related to eye movements, there are certain treatments that you can opt for.

Lens: At times, using therapeutic lenses can help in the improvement of someone's eye movements. As an individual observes background or peripheral objects, lenses can help in refining their focus.

Vision therapy: Such therapy can also be used for treating problems in eye movements.

Syntonic: In this method, various colored lights are used to adjust the problems of eye movements in a person.

Comprehension

There are various strategies that can be followed for comprehending any kind of matter. Readers need to connect with the already acquired information or knowledge from other texts or things from the world. A reader will need to combine their knowledge with the new info or ideas in order to understand the actual text meanings, new thinking ways, or some new creative style. You, as a reader, will be making all kinds of questions in your mind in relation to the text. Most of the questions will be based on your effective reaction after you are done with reading the text and for the purpose the writer has written the text.

Reading Comprehension

Reading comprehension is all about an action of properly understanding the matter that is being read. It plays an essential role as you read something. It will need activeness, intension, and information processing from your side before you start to read any kind of text, as you read something, and also after you are done with reading. Comprehension is the last aspect of the action of reading. There are two elements that play the most important role in processing reading comprehension. They are vocabulary knowledge and text comprehension. Also, your capability to understand the applied vocabulary within some text acts as an essential factor. When your vocabulary knowledge is not that great, you will need to keep learning new words.

In fact, it is important to understand the intended meaning of every word within a section of text. You can put the meaning of the words in one place so that you can form some meaningful concept that is being explained within the text. Comprehension is often regarded as the basic goal of reading as well as listening. It provides readers and listeners all the help to gain knowledge and skills. Typically, there are four types of reading - intensive, skimming, extensive, and scanning. Out of all these, the easiest one is skimming. It is similar to taking one glance at the presented matter. Scanning is slightly more meticulous in nature and is put into use when readers try to search for some particular matter in the text.

The process of intensive reading is more interspersed with the concept of comprehension. If a reader decides to follow the intensive reading, he/she will need to read all the words that are present within the text. The reader will need to look out for the meaning of the words that are unfamiliar in nature. It is important to understand the text's meaning thoroughly by connecting with the text. It is the ideal form of reading when the reader needs to explain the meaning or thoughts of the text with his/her speech or writing. When readers read any kind of text for the sake of pleasure, they can opt for extensive reading. If it is possible for you to practice reading comprehension on a daily basis, your overall skill to understand comprehension will get improved.

For instance, practicing reading comprehension can help a student to develop a great career in academics. When anyone finds it tough to read comprehension, the probable reasons are fewer ideas, less vocabulary knowledge, and various other nuances. You can opt for several ways to enhance your skills of reading comprehension. They are comprehension monitoring, collaborative learning, question answering, question generation, story structure, and summarization. Comprehension monitoring is a metacognitive process that includes two methods. They are regulation and evaluation by understanding the presented text. When someone reads together in a group, it shows collaborative learning. At times, an individual reads a text portion and then analyzes the question pattern that might be asked. The reader will be able to formulate the answers, and it is all about question answering.

Speed Reading Is All About Concentration

It is necessary to enhance your skills when it comes to reading, irrespective of the profession you are involved with. In case there is any need to make reports, periodicals, proposals, and letters for your work, speed reading is necessary. It can provide you all the help to save a lot of time. Additionally, it will let you develop your skills of concentration. Some of the definite ways of enhancing your level of concentration are:

Staying away from distractions: You need to eliminate distractions to focus on the text you are reading. In order to do this, you can switch off the TV, radio, or phone. Also, you can opt for some quiet place so that you can improve your concentration while reading.

Being trained to avoid rereading: You can easily provide yourself with all the necessary training so that you can avoid rereading the previous texts. You need to practice reading every sentence for one time without mistakes of any kind. You can cover all those lines that you have read using your hands or an index card. Keep dragging it down on the page as you read it. Such a technique will let you read properly while enhancing your speed of reading.

Controlling your speed of reading: The reading speed that you have might vary, depending on the material categories that you are reading. Your materials for reading can be a newspaper or a magazine. You can opt for reading only the necessary info or headlines. Skimming the essential sections can help you to enhance your speed of reading.

As you read anything related to science or mathematics, you are required to be even more attentive. Also, you will have to read in detail as it can help better understand the matter. You will need to judge on your own the subject priorities. It can help in developing your speed of reading by making some adjustments in your reading patterns.

Benefits of Speed Reading

There are various benefits of reading with speed. Let's have a look at some of them.

You can read more volume that too within less amount of time. As you try to read faster, it can help in reading a huge amount of text within a very short time period. So, if you have less time in hand, and you need to finish a big portion of text, speed reading can help you get through it.

You will have a better understanding as you will be reading with perfection and greater depth. As you try to read something with all your focus, you can easily read with greater depth and perfection. It can help you to understand the meaning of the text in a much better way.

You will need to involve a higher level of concentration for reading any kind of text at a fast speed. It will let you concentrate on the concept almost instantly.

As you read something with all your attention, it can help in keeping the info in your mind.

You will get the chance to read various types of texts as you read with speed. It can easily satisfy your mind if you are someone who loves to read.

Some of the other benefits of speed reading are:

You can shop quickly by having a look at the information that is available on the nutrition label.

You can quickly go through the instructions while assembling or operating any item.

Speed reading can help in improving your career. It can provide you all the help that is needed to perform any kind of desk job within a work environment in an efficient way. As you get done with all your work on time, you can receive promotions and rewards.

How to Maximize Comprehension?

It is quite essential to learn about the ways in which you can read and comprehend any kind of text properly. As you maximize your skills of comprehension, you can get efficiency and pleasure for work. Here are certain ways in which you can maximize your skills of comprehension for reading any kind of text.

Choosing a productive time

You will need to think of the time when you like the most to perform any kind of work while involving all your effort. It might be early in the morning, mid-day, or at night. You need to select a particular time to read your desired texts so that you can maximize all your skills of comprehension.

Choosing a productive place

You need to find out a productive place where you would like to read. It can be your room, library, café, office, and any other place. You need to select a place where you can sit comfortably and set up your mind for reading.

Staying away from all kinds of distractions

Before you decide to start reading, you need to free yourself from all kinds of distractions. You can also ask others not to disturb you during your reading time.

Conclusion

As you have finished this guidebook, now it is time to apply each of the steps that you have found here. Try to practice reading more as it can serve you in two ways. It will not only enhance your reading skills, but you will also be able to learn new words that can enhance your vocabulary. Once you are done with the basics, just keep practicing, as that is the only thing that can take you to the next level. Indeed, it is not possible to be a speed reader overnight. But with consistency and dedication, you can easily master the skills with time. Speed reading can be regarded as a genuine reading upgrade. It will not only help you in saving time, but it will also be enhancing your awareness. The tips and tricks that have been included in this guidebook are easy to follow. Make sure that you do not rush things. Take your time to enhance your reading speed.